YOUR KNOWLEDGE HAS VALUE

- We will publish your bachelor's and master's thesis, essays and papers

- Your own eBook and book - sold worldwide in all relevant shops

- Earn money with each sale

Upload your text at www.GRIN.com
and publish for free

Bibliographic information published by the German National Library:

The German National Library lists this publication in the National Bibliography; detailed bibliographic data are available on the Internet at http://dnb.dnb.de .

This book is copyright material and must not be copied, reproduced, transferred, distributed, leased, licensed or publicly performed or used in any way except as specifically permitted in writing by the publishers, as allowed under the terms and conditions under which it was purchased or as strictly permitted by applicable copyright law. Any unauthorized distribution or use of this text may be a direct infringement of the author s and publisher s rights and those responsible may be liable in law accordingly.

Imprint:

Copyright © 2018 GRIN Verlag
Print and binding: Books on Demand GmbH, Norderstedt Germany
ISBN: 9783346117069

This book at GRIN:

https://www.grin.com/document/513849

Novi Kesumaningtyas

User Interface Design of the Triage Health App

GRIN Verlag

GRIN - Your knowledge has value

Since its foundation in 1998, GRIN has specialized in publishing academic texts by students, college teachers and other academics as e-book and printed book. The website www.grin.com is an ideal platform for presenting term papers, final papers, scientific essays, dissertations and specialist books.

Visit us on the internet:

http://www.grin.com/

http://www.facebook.com/grincom

http://www.twitter.com/grin_com

FIT5152 Assignment 4

Digital Prototyping Assignment

Followed Design Guidelines in Mobile Triage App Prototype

Novi Kesumaningtyas

Executive Summary

Triage App is a mobile application that helps nurse/paramedics to sort patients based on their need for immediate treatment according to certain guidelines. Using the app, users can simply report their current patients' conditions as the app label their Triage status and store them to the database. For this functionality, we assumed that the system already has patient details that can be retrieved from the unique patient ID number. The app also allows users to search and view details of their patients along with the visualization of their current locations on Triage App's map.

Accordingly, an iOS digital prototype that provides a better idea of how the product will look like has been created. The purpose of this report is to provide an explanatory on the design guidelines that we have followed in creating Triage App user interface prototype. This is highlighted on our designed screens that reflect Triage App main features, namely Sign-up/Sign-in, User Profile, Edit User Profile, SIEVE Triage, Search by a Patient, Multicriteria Search, Reports and Maps. On each of these screens a minimum of four guidelines for user interface design that mainly stated by Norman (2013) and Nielsen (1995) are described. This includes guidelines for navigation, form, button, colour, feedback, layout, error messages and correction, so that discoverability and visibility can be achieved. By following these guidelines, the Triage App is expected to deliver its functionalities for potential users in a more effective way.

Based on our analysis on such guidelines, design principles that cover feedback inclusion such as error message or system loading message, are mostly appropriate for mobile form design. Therefore, the guidelines were applied in our UI design for sign in/sign up, user profile, search and map forms. Another design guideline principle that prominently applied and implemented in our design is the aesthetic and minimalist design as suggested by Nielsen (1995) in his heuristic principles for system usability.

Table of Contents

Executive Summary 2
Design Guidelines 4
    1.   Sign-in and Sign-up Page 4
    2.   User profile page 7
    3.   Edit Profile page 9
    4.   SIEVE Triage page 11
    5.   Search Page 13
    6.   Report Page 15
    7.   Map Page 17
References 19
Appendix 20

Design Guidelines

In designing the prototype for Triage App, we used several design guidelines about discoverability principles (Norman, 2013), iOS navigation, menus and mobile form design as described in the following sub-sections.

1. Sign-in and Sign-up Page

In Triage App, sign in and sign up screen plays a pivotal role as it is the first screen being shown when user opening the app.
Followed design guidelines:

1. Make things clear and simple
2. Provide hint text using appropriate design pattern
3. Reduce memory load and use cognitive aids (an option if the password is forgotten, an option to keep the user sign in, give user options to hide/show entered password)
4. Use clear error messages
5. Error correction: refocus on the field containing the error

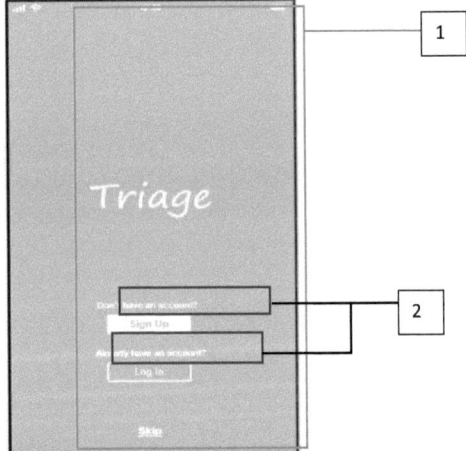

Figure 1. Sign up and Sign in page

When designing this screen, we want to make sure that the three options available to access the app (sign up if they don't have a Triage account, sign in if they already have an account, or skip these two options and log in as a guest user instead) are clearly visible for the user. Therefore, to achieve this goal, we followed Norman (2013)'s design guideline on *making things clear and simple* by adding proper hint texts as *signifiers* and showing these three options only on a single screen as can be seen on Figure 1 above. Even so, to indicate the importance of each of the three options, each of them is designed differently. Sign up option that allows user to create a Triage account is shown firstly and in a white box, log in option that enables user to log in and access all features provided in Triage App is shown secondly in a box that has same colour with the background and in white text colour, while skip option that allows guest user to access information stored in Triage App is shown lastly with an underlined text format to inform user that it is also clickable even though unlike the other two options, it has no box.

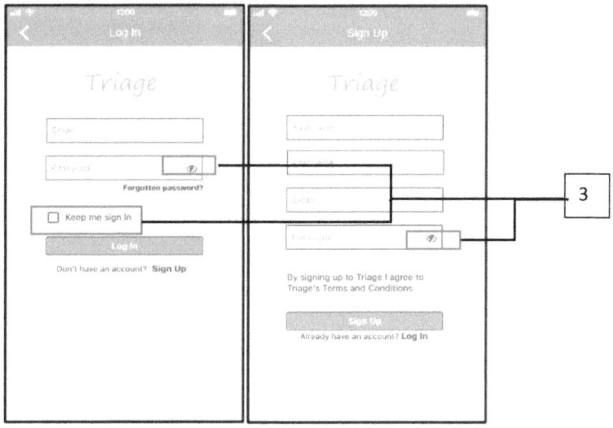

Figure 2. Triage App sign in and sign up form

Hint/helper texts that act as signifiers also used in both sign in and sign up forms. As can be seen on Figure 2 above, each of data entry boxes on both forms has a grey text that signals user to write on them and describes the kind of information needed for each field. Meanwhile, as suggested by Norman (2013), in creating an interaction design, we need to *reduce memory load and use cognitive aids* for the users. So, in purpose of fulfilling this guideline, on our design we also included Neil's (2014) and Wroblewski's (2015) design suggestions about the inclusion of an option for users if they forgot their password on sign in screen, an option to remember the password so that they do not have to recall it the next time they want to log in, an option to keep them signed in, and an option to show or hide their entered password so that they can both check if they entered the right password and can hide it on sign in and sign up screens as can be seen on Figure 2.

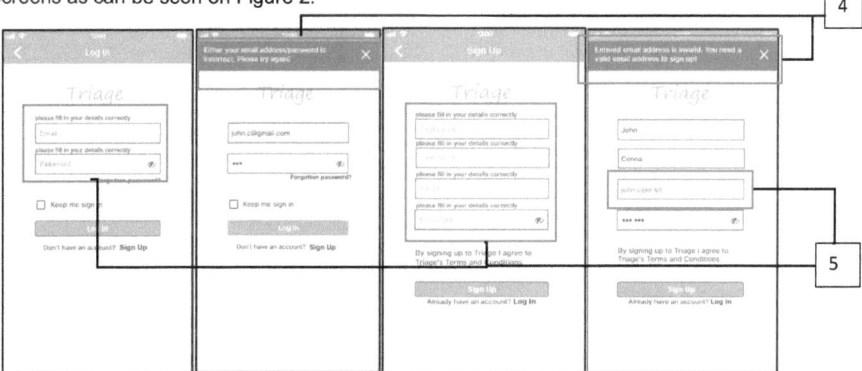

Figure 3. Error feedbacks on Triage App's sign in and sign up forms

In addition to that, we also provide error messages as an immediate feedback for users whenever they made mistakes on the sign in or sign up data entry forms. As can be seen on Figure 3 above, when a wrong/incomplete data entry is entered, the field containing the error is also highlighted with a red mark when a wrong input is entered. This is based on Neil (2014) design guideline on mobile forms to always include clear error messages and provide error correction for the user.

2. User profile page

The User Profile page provides a user interface screen that allows user entering their personal details to create a new account profile. This screen can be accessed only after a user's first and name along with their valid email address and a chosen password are successfully submitted in the last sign up page.

Followed design guidelines:
1. *Strive for consistency*
2. *Aesthetic and minimalist design*
3. *Recognition rather than recall*
4. *Placing buttons where they are easy to access*
5. *Provide the user with the feedback on the current status and progress*

After the sign-up task is successfully performed, the screen will welcome the user by their first name and show a text that engage user to start their profile as can be seen on Figure 4. This is then also shown continually on each steps of User Profile screen where in user's personal details need to be entered. The continuous welcome message and consistent layout design were intentionally included to follow Shneiderman's (2014) guideline to *strive for consistency* in designing a product interface. Meanwhile, to avoid cluttering and keeping *an aesthetic and minimalist design* (Nielsen, 1995) the data entry forms are split into three pages with a page control being used as the navigation. The inclusion of page control is based on iOS Navigation Guidelines that suggest the use of a page control when there are multiple pages of the same type of content in a product user interface (Google.com, n.d.).

Figure 4. Data entry form for user profile details

As shown on the Figure 4 above, the first page of this User Profile screen is the job position field, in which user can enter their current profession around health and medical field. To limit the data entry so that user can only input such medical profession, a pre-determined list that referred to health and medical job positions is shown when user click/type on the data entry field. While the list constraints job position data entry to the health and medical job positions only, at the same time it also helps user reduce their short-term memory load. This is also what we intended when designing this User Profile section, as based on Nielsen's (1995) design usability principle to emphasize on *user's recognition rather than recall*.

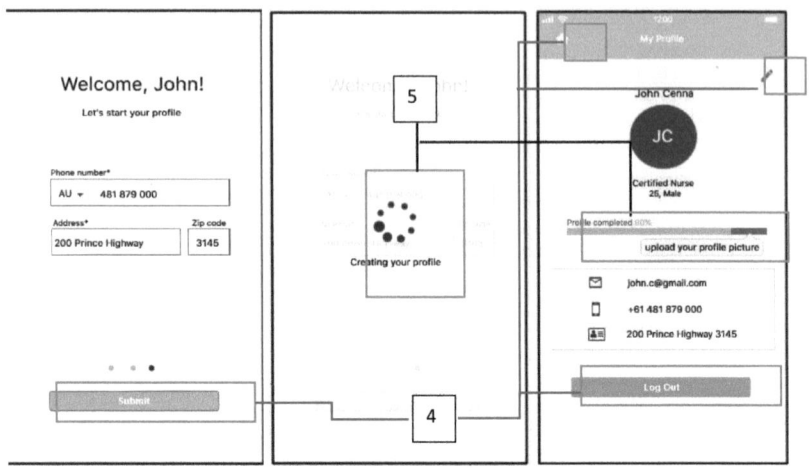

Figure 5. Finishing user profile data entry

To facilitate the operability of the User Profile data entry, the submit button that allows all entered profile details to be stored and thus creating a new user account/profile, is placed on the bottom of the page right under the page control navigation where user's thumb is usually placed. This was intentionally designed to facilitate user access to the button (Web Accessibility Initiative, n.d.). Even so, as can be seen on Figure 4 and Figure 5, the colour of the submit button is different when the fields are being populated and empty. The lighter colour for the submit button was created so that user can know that the button is unclickable and user profile could not be created if marked (*) fields are still empty. Whereas, when all required data entries are entered, as an immediate feedback, the colour of the button is changed into a darker colour spectrum to signal to user that it is now clickable. Another feedback also provided after the submit button is clicked as can be seen on Figure 5. To communicate the result of the 'submit' action, the screen then will show a loading icon with a text that says 'creating your profile' to *provide the user with the feedback on the current status and progress* (Neil, 2014). After the process is completed, a page titled as 'My Profile' then showed to indicate that a user profile has been successfully created.

3. Edit Profile page

After a new account has been successfully created from the sign-up task and user profile data entry, user can still personalise or modify their details through this Edit Profile page that can be accessed from 'My Profile'. From the Edit Profile page, user can also upload their profile picture and change their current password into a new one.

Followed design guidelines:
1. Vertical labelling (Neil, 2014)
2. Provide hint text using appropriate design pattern (Neil, 2014)
3. Make affordances visible (Norman, 2013)
4. Logical grouping and sequencing of fields (Neil, 2014)
5. Provide an immediate feedback after an action has been performed (Norman, 2013)

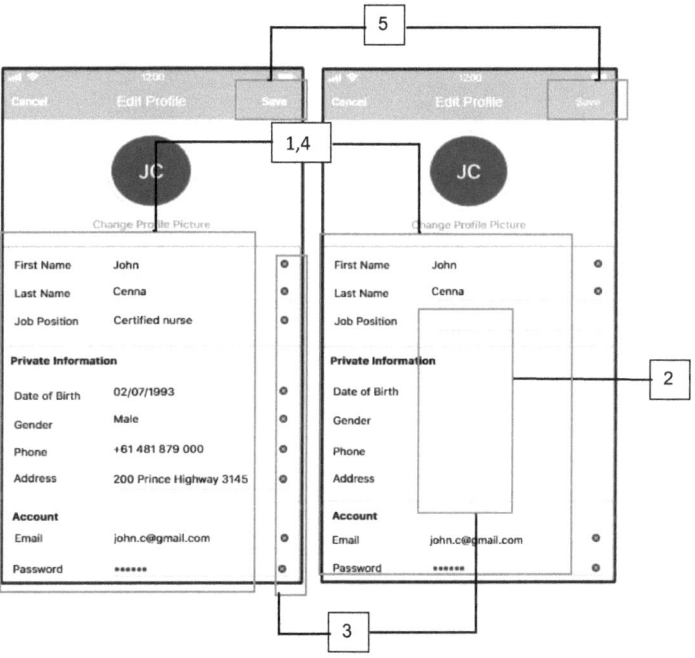

Figure 6. Edit profile form

To enable user modifying their profile details, a vertical labelled form that grouped and sequence user details' fields is used to *provide better spacing and visual flow* in the Edit Profile UI page (Neil, 2014) as can be seen on Figure 6 above. Meanwhile, on the page header it can be seen that there are three texts being described: 'Cancel', 'Edit Profile' and 'Save'. For both 'Cancel' and 'Save', a slightly smaller text size was used to differentiate their functions from the 'Edit Profile' text that acted as the title of this page form. However, on the form where in not all data fields are being populated, a lighter spectrum of colour is used to signal the affordances of the text has been changed from clickable to unclickable. This is intended to avoid incomplete user details that can cause poor data quality on the user profile information, in case that accidental modifying was concurred on this Edit Profile screen. At the same time, the change of colour on the 'save' button also acts as a feedback whenever a data field is erased/emptied.

In addition to that, to enable the form's discoverability, a signifier icon also added on each populated field so that user can know that these fields are editable. To highlight the actions that can be done on these editable fields even more, each of them is equipped with a help text describing additional guidance for the field's supposed input.

4. SIEVE Triage page

SIEVE Triage is one of main functionalities provided in Triage App. It allows nurse/paramedic to sort their patients based on their current condition severity and needs for a treatment. To perform the SIEVE task through this feature, users need to enter their patient id number first, by which allowing the system to find the patient details on Triage's back-end database. After a valid Patient ID is entered, the system then retrieves the patient's details and shows the patient full name on the screen along with a list of fields in which users can input the patient's condition details to sort his/her Triage label for the treatment.

Followed design guidelines:
1. Always provide a clear path
2. Logical grouping/sequencing of fields
3. Reduce visual clutter
4. Optional and required fields clearly marked
5. Provide immediate feedback

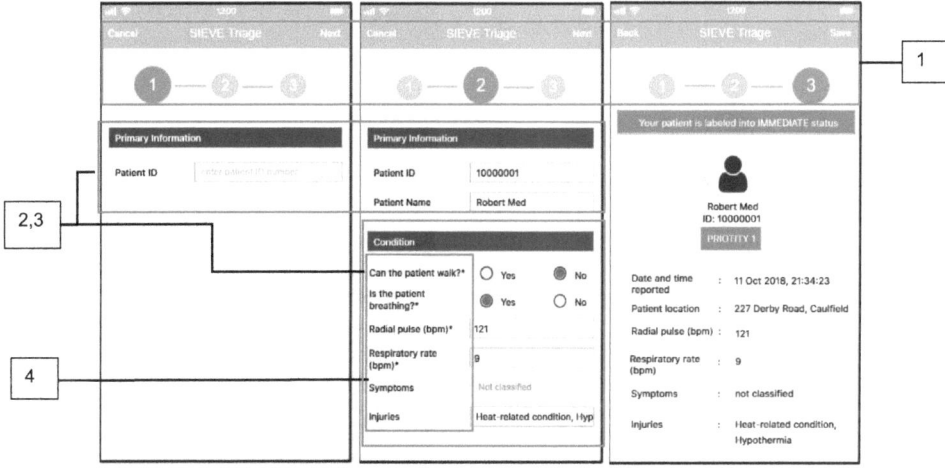

Figure 7. Steps needed in SIEVE page

In designing SIEVE interface pages, we wanted to show users that there will be three steps needed to perform this functionality. Accordingly, on the top pages of SIEVE task interface, we added three numbered circles that signal which step the user is in while they can navigate to continue or cancel the task by clicking on 'next' or 'cancel' button on the page's header as can be seen on Figure 7 above. Such design was created based on iOS Navigation guideline that suggest UI designers to *always provide a clear path for the user* (Google.com, n.d.). Thus, we also include 'SIEVE Triage' as the title of the page on its header as a way to inform user that they are still performing SIEVE Triage task. Whilst, to communicate the affordances of 'next'/'save' and 'cancel'/'back' that they are clickable and can be used to navigate them to SIEVE next/previous step, we set their text size to be slightly smaller than the title of the pages.

By sequencing SIEVE task into three steps, we can group the data entry fields in a logical manner without cluttering the UI screen, thus complying on Neil's (2014) design guideline to group related items in a mobile form design so that it would not confuse user with cluttered fields of form. In addition to that, as can be seen on Figure 7, an asterisk (*) mark also included to differentiate required and optional data entry fields. This then complies Shneiderman (2014)'s guideline to have optional and required fields clearly marked on a form design.

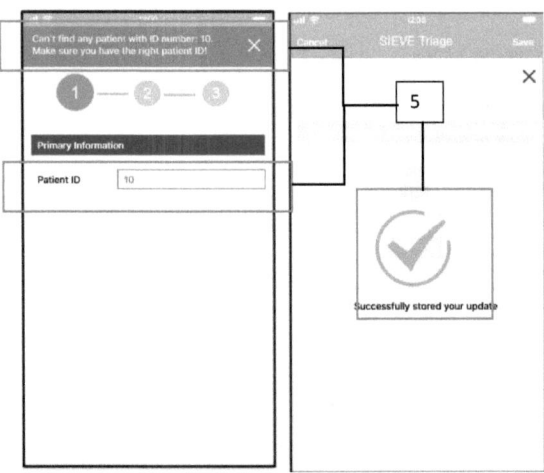

Figure 8. Feedback: error message & correction, progress/completion message

Meanwhile, according to Norman's (2013) design guidelines, an immediate feedback is needed to increase the visibility and discoverability of a project, while Shneiderman (2014) also suggest that in a form design, there should always be a completion feedback. Thus, as can be seen on Figure 8, after a SIEVE label is shown and 'save' button is selected, the screen will provide a feedback message that signal SIEVE task is successfully performed and the data is stored into Triage App database. In addition to that, an error message and correction is also suggested as a feedback for when user make mistakes in a form design (Neil, 2014). accordingly, as can be seen on the figure above, if a wrong patient ID is entered, the screen will then show a message that indicate such error, along with a highlighted red colour on the field containing the error.

5. Search Page

There are two search pages in Triage App. The first search page is to search by patient's detail and the second is search by the combination of Triage label, symptom, and injury. This search page is meant to show the specific patients without user needs to go through all patients result in one by one. That is why these search pages need to be as clear as possible for the user to use.

Followed guidelines:
1. Mobile guidelines for Fixed Tabs (Google.com, n.d)
2. The design of everyday things guidelines: Feedback (Norman, 2013)
3. The design of everyday things guidelines: Mapping (Norman, 2013)
4. The design of everyday things guidelines: Constraints (Norman, 2013)

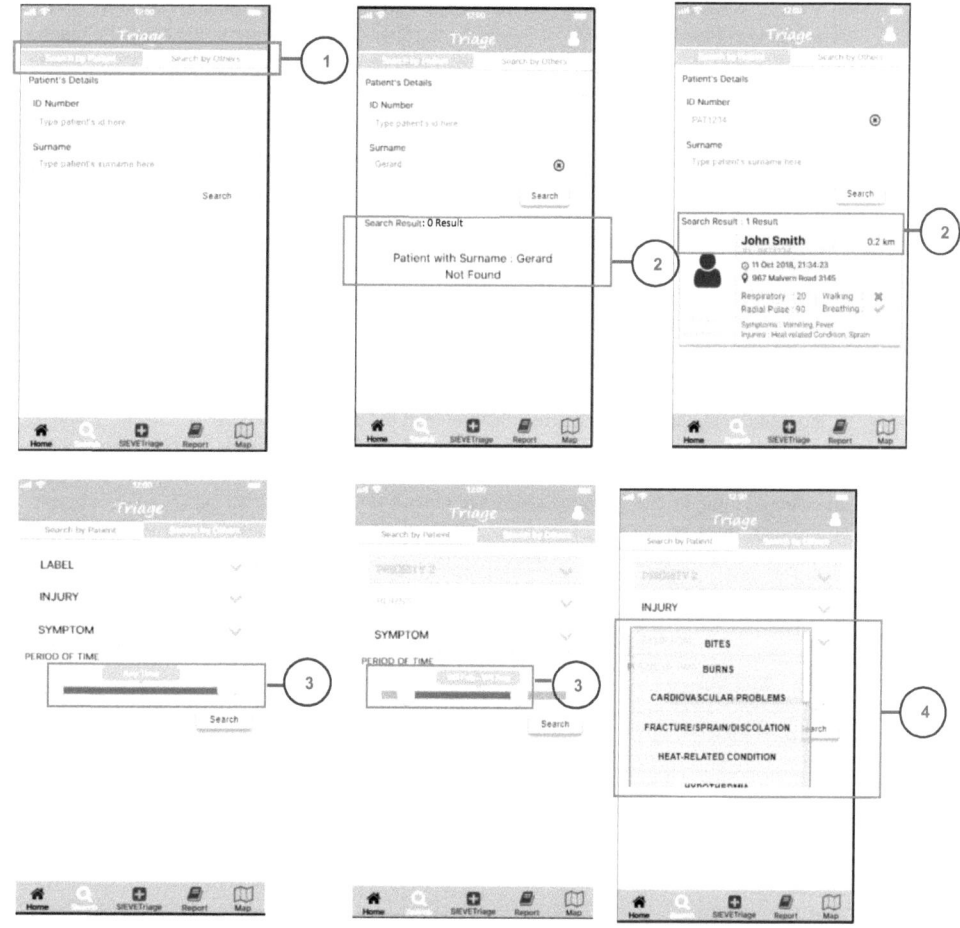

Figure 9. Search page interface

At the top of the search page, there is a fixed tab that shows 'Search by Patient' and 'Search by Others'. 'Search by Patient' tab will let user search patient's detail by input patient's ID or patient's surname while 'Search by Others' will let user search by patient's label, symptom, injury, and the period for the time of patient's data input. We never know what filter that user wants to search for the patients, it creates the condition where the user needs to see these search function at the same time. That means that both search functions are equally important. Also, based on the mobile guidelines for the fixed tab, if the number of options is limited, and options are viewed frequently, then a fixed tab can be used. These search functions are fulfilled criteria that fixed tab has, so the fixed tab is suitable for the search function in this page.

After the user inputs the data and clicks on the search button, then the result will come based on the user input. There will be feedback to let the user aware of how many data found based on the user input. So user knows that the system has processed the request they have given. Based on Don Norman guideline for feedback, feedback is used for communicating the results of an action and letting the user know that the system is working. The search function in Triage app will let the user knows the result of their search request immediately even if the system found no result.

At the 'Search by Others' tab, the user can set the period of patients input data. The user can set the period through the scroll bar that has two adjustable circles on each edge. If a user moves the left side circle, then the start period will move forward to the current week and if the user moves the right side circle, then the end period will move to the past week. Based on the Don Norman guideline for mapping, the user should able to identify the mapping between the elements clearly and efficiently. To show what will happen if the user moves the circles, there will be a tooltip above the scroll bar to show that the scroll bar and the period has a relationship between each other. The adjustable circle will control the length of period that will show in the result.

At the 'Search by Others' tab, the user also able to set the label, symptoms and injury. Based on the Don Norman guideline, constraints can limit the set of possible actions given by the user. In other words, it means to prevent the error that might arise if the user gives the unexpected input to the system. Depart from that, I put the dropdown list on each category, so the user does not have to type by themselves. Moreover, because the answers already provided, then the system will not get the unexpected answer from the user.

6. Report Page

Report page is used for display the total patients according to their triage label. The users can see the report in the form of pie chart and bar graph.

Followed guidelines:
1. Vertical labelling for mobile design (Neil, 2014)
2. Icon Signifiers (Google.com, n.d.)
3. The design of everyday things guidelines: Mapping (Norman, 2013)
4. Visibility of system status (Nielsen, 1995)

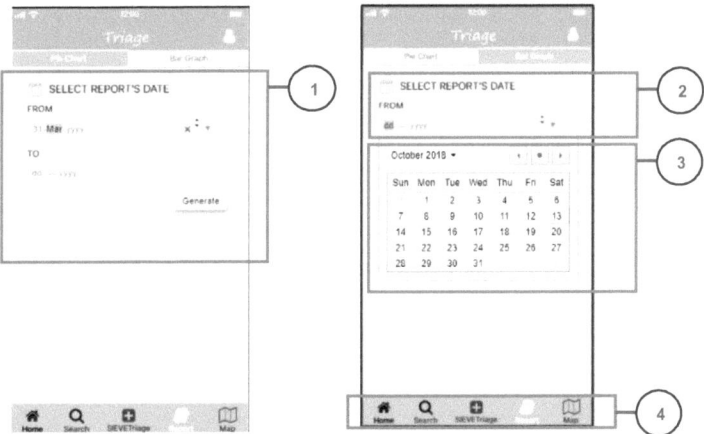

Figure 10. Report page interface

In the report section, user able to set the period of the report on their mobile phone. From Mobile Forms Design Strategies by Chui Chui Tan (Tan, 2011) stated that mobile forms need to be more efficient and simple because the screen size of mobile phones is relatively small if we compared with the computer screen. The mobile user generally scrolls to the bottom to look for more information rather than scroll horizontally. That is why vertical labelling is more suitable for a mobile phone because it can give better spacing and better visual flow. By this way, we can avoid labels truncated or overlapping each other if users' mobile screen size is smaller than the model mobile screen size that developer use to design the application.

Based on Material Design that described anatomy text field (Google.com, n.d) we can use icon signifiers to describe to the user what is the type of input and action that we expect from the user. When the user reads the title to select the report's date, there is a calendar icon beside the label to give user clue that the app expects the user to give a specific date for the report. In the text box, there is a 'V' icon to give a hint to the user there will be something come up if the user clicks the button. This drop-down icon is also able to give a clue to the user that they need to click the icon to fill the textbox.

After the user clicked the drop-down 'V' icon, they will able to see the calendar. In the top side of the calendar, there are left '<' and right '>' control icons. By seeing this, the user can expect that these buttons are used for moving the selected square on the calendar also by selecting this date the textbox will automatically fill by the selected date without user need to type by themselves. Based on Mapping by Don Norman (Norman, 2013) when the relationship between control and the objects are obvious, we do not need to add labels and instruction to the controller which is called Natural Mapping. By giving the common left and right icon ('<' '>') to the user, I expect that user can grasp what the icon means without the need to put the instruction label beside it.

Nielsen's Usability Heuristic (Nielsen, 1995) stated that the example of good practice of visibility of system status is every page should be able to indicate where the user is. Depart from this guideline I put different contrast colour in the navigation bar that indicates that the page that user access at that moment. The icon at the navigation page will change from black colour to the white colour if user open that page, by this way user always know which page that they are now working currently.

7. Map Page

The map page will show the markers that present the patients' Triage location based on the location that user input in the form.

Followed guidelines:
1. Error message – Assistive element from Material Design (Google.com, n.d.)
2. Error Prevention (Nielsen, 1995)
3. The design of everyday things guidelines: feedback (Norman, 2013)
4. Aesthetic and minimalist design (Nielsen, 1995)

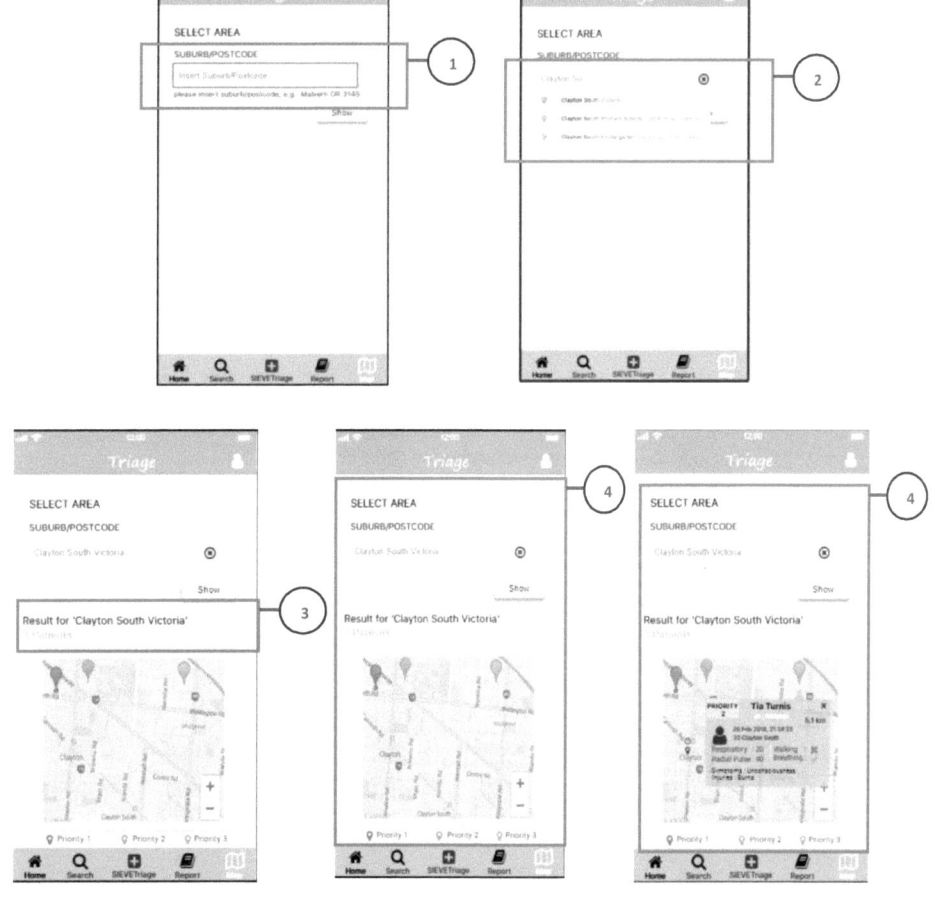

Figure 11. Map page interface

The map page expects the user to give input in the textbox. Based on the error message guideline (Google.com, n.d) if the user gives unexpected input to the system, we can give an error message to display instruction on how to fix it so the system can work as it should be. There will be an error message shown if the user directly clicks show without insert any suburb or postcode at the textbox. In the error message, there is also an example to give user hint how to fill the textbox.

Besides the error message, Nielsen's 10 Heuristic (Nielsen, 1995) also stated that the proper user interface should able to have error prevention on the page. This objective can be obtained by having a design that provides a helpful suggestion to the user. When user input the suburb/postcode there will be suggestion shows on the textbox to give constraint on the user input. The user does not need to type everything by themselves, they can choose by the suggestion and convince themselves that the input they are given is correct.

After the user clicks the 'Show' button, there will be a map and also feedback that says the map shows the result for particular suburb/postcode that the user is has given and how many patients located in that area. Based on the Norman guideline for feedback (Norman, 2013) user need the feedback to let themselves aware that the system has been accepting their request and work like the user expect too. By this feedback, I expect user will understand that by giving the input of suburb/postcode to the system they can get a map in that location including how many patients are there where every marker in that map indicates the patients' Triage label.

For the example of good user interface design, Nielsen's 10 Heuristics stated that aesthetic and minimalist design is better for the user. That means that the user can focus to the main point that the app tries to provide to the user. Based on this guideline I made map page as simple as possible. The user does not need to move to another page to see the result or to see the detail of the patient. Everything is on one page. The user also does not need to type the full address to get the result. They only need to type whether postcode or suburb in the same text box and the suggestion will show for both. White colour as a background colour also shows a simplicity for the design. The use of contrast colour in the page like black colour makes it easier for the user to differentiate the main words because it is not overlapping with the background colour. The user will expect to see the map when they navigate to the Map page, and that is what exactly they will see on this page without any irrelevant information.

References

Google.com (n.d.). *Tabs*. Retrieved from Material Design: https://material.io/design/components/#

Lee, Y. E., & Benbasat, I. (2003). Interface design for mobile commerce. *Communications of the ACM, 46(12)* (pp. 48-52). ACM.

Malkov, G. V., & Kruglov, A. (June, 2018). Peculiarities of Development of the Mobile Software for Log Batch Volume Measurement. *Proceedings of the 2018 International Conference on Control and Computer Vision* (pp. 115-120). ACM.

Neil, T. (2014). Mobile design pattern gallery: UI patterns for smartphone apps. O'Reilly Media, Inc.

Nielsen, J. (1995). *10 usability heuristics for user interface design.* Nielsen Norman Group, 1(1).

Norman, D. (2013). *The design of everyday things: Revised and expanded edition.* Constellation.

Shneiderman, Plasiant, Cohen and Jacobs *(2014) Designing the User Interface: Strategies for Effective Human-Computer Interaction, 5thEdition. Pearson.*

Tan, C. C. (2011, March 15). *Mobile form design strategies*. Retrieved from uxbooth: http://www.uxbooth.com/articles/mobile-form-design-strategies/

Web Accessibility Initiative. (n.d.) *Mobile Accessibility Mapping.* https://www.w3.org/TR/mobile-accessibility-mapping/

Wroblewski, L. (2015). *Showing Passwords on Log-In Screens.* Available at: http://lukew.com/ff/entry.asp?1941

Zamzami, I., & Mahmud, M. (2012, November). User satisfaction on smartphone interface design, information quality evaluation. *Advanced Computer Science Applications and Technologies (ACSAT), 2012 International Conference on* (pp. 78-82). IEEE.

Appendix

Triage App Site Map

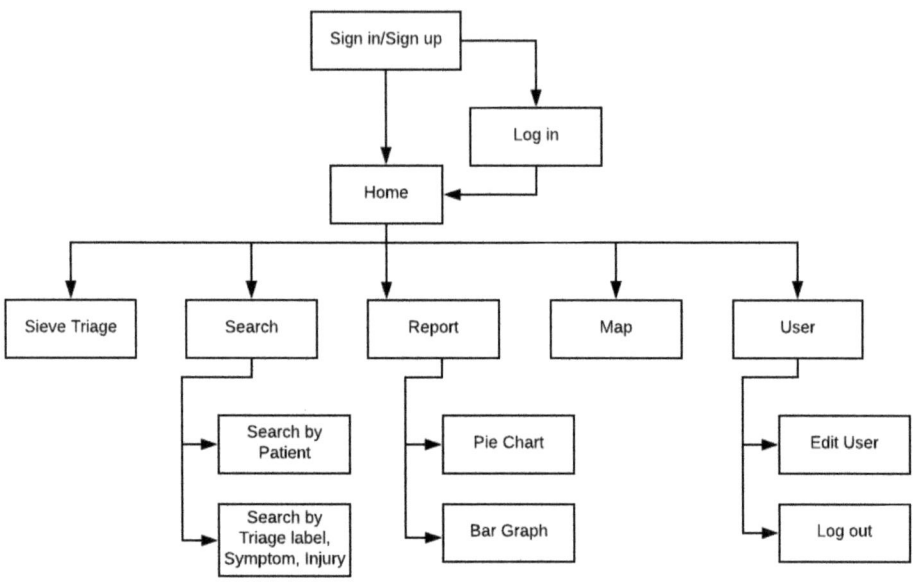

YOUR KNOWLEDGE HAS VALUE

- We will publish your bachelor's and master's thesis, essays and papers

- Your own eBook and book - sold worldwide in all relevant shops

- Earn money with each sale

Upload your text at www.GRIN.com
and publish for free